CW00602085

Blue Mountains

NEW SOUTH WALES

PASCAL
PRESS

DISCOVERING
THE BLUE MOUNTAINS

Sixty-five kilometres west of Sydney, the Blue Mountains parts its shimmering veil to reveal the beauty of its sculptured cliffs and forested valleys. The Great Western Highway snakes along the top of this fantastically eroded plateau, providing easy access to breathtaking scenery, charming villages and outstanding bushwalking country. This premier tourist destination is renowned for its fine restaurants, colonial architecture and seasonal garden festivals.

Over 200,000 hectares of the mountains' sandstone escarpments and deep river valleys are reserved as national park. An excellent walking-track system takes visitors from ridge-top woodlands and heaths down into hidden worlds of rainforest, rockpools and towering eucalypt forests.

The Blue Mountains impart a sense of wonder to all who experience the heady mountain air and majestic splendour.

Opposite:
The Three Sisters overlook the Jamison Valley at Katoomba.

Left:
The Mountain Devil, floral emblem of the Blue Mountains.

LIFE IN THE MOUNTAINS

The Blue Mountains have been luring people to their lofty heights for over 100 years. There are those who come for a day or a week, while the enchanted make their home here. The mountains are a magnet for artists and writers seeking inspiration in nature. Other inspired residents have created magnificent exotic gardens that thrive in this highland climate.

Each of the 24 towns scattered along the plateau has its special attractions highlighting the history and natural beauty of the region. Katoomba, with its cable car, cliff-top lookouts and walking tracks, makes an ideal base for exploring the wonders of the Blue Mountains.

Pages 4–5:
A scenic drive links ridge-top towns.

Opposite, top:
Katoomba sits above the Jamison Valley.

Opposite, bottom:
Leura Mall attracts tourists with it's quaint stores.

Left:
Cliff-top lookouts offer stunning vistas.

MORNINGS IN THE MIST

A feeling of isolation pervades the Blue Mountains on those special mornings when the sandstone parapets float on a sea of mist. The echoing call of the lyrebird rises from shrouded valleys as reluctant commuters head for the city.

Viewed from Sydney, the plateau is a distant blue haze, created by sunlight filtering through mountain air filled with fine droplets of eucalyptus oil. As the work-weary return to their Blue Mountain retreats, the setting sun ignites the western escarpments.

Pages 8–9:
The Three Sisters cling to the cliffs above the Jamison Valley.

Right:
Blue Mountains magic.

Opposite:
Waves of mist lap the cliff faces.

WILDLIFE ENCOUNTERS

The Blue Mountains are a haven for Australian native animals. Surveying vast territories, lone birds of prey soar above the cliffs. In the cool, damp forests below, Platypus, water dragons, Golden Whistlers and Spotted-tailed Quolls all find a niche. Koalas, Eastern Grey Kangaroos and Sugar Gliders prefer the open forests and woodlands, where sweet-scented flowers and bushland fruits attract flocks of colourful parrots.

Pages 12–13:
The Campbell Rhododendron Gardens at Blackheath.

Opposite:
A male Australian King-Parrot.

Left:
Crimson Rosella.

FALLING WATER

Water, in its guises of rain, snow, frost and trickling creeks, is the creative force that shapes the Blue Mountains and sustains their lifeforms. It weathers the soft sandstones and shales into sheer-walled cliffs and narrow chasms.

There are numerous locations where visitors can admire the handiwork of tributaries feeding the Coxs, Grose and Nepean Rivers as they plunge from the escarpments. The National Pass walking track takes visitors over and under the cliffs around Wentworth Falls. Other trails follow cascading creeks and fern-filled gorges to the valley floors.

Pages 16–17:
An abundance of woodland — Grose Valley.

Opposite:
The tranquil tracery of Wentworth Falls.

Left:
Leura Cascades.

Pages 20–21:
Delicate ferns shelter in rainforest gullies.

CHANGING SEASONS

Cool-climate plants from Asia and the Northern Hemisphere flourish in the Blue Mountains. In autumn, the magic touch of frost paints gardens and parks in fiery colours as fallen leaves carpet country lanes.

Early flowering natives see out the last of winter's cold days and mountain towns begin preparing a festive welcome for spring. The Blackheath Rhododendron Festival at Bacchante Gardens is a highlight of the many spring garden festivals held throughout the Blue Mountains.

Opposite:
A resting place in the Norman Lindsay Gallery and Museum gardens.

Left:
Autumn colours blanket the gardens.

RECALLING THE PAST

The Blue Mountains presented a formidable barrier to the westward expansion of colonial New South Wales. It took some 25 years of trial and error before an official route across the mountains was established in 1813.

During the 1870s, luxury hotels and guesthouses began catering for Sydney's elite who enjoyed the benefits of "taking the air". The completion of a rail line to Mt Victoria in 1876 provided affordable access for all. By the 1930s, the Blue Mountains had become a mecca for intrepid bushwalkers and daring rock-climbers.

Today, visiting historic sites is as much a part of the Blue Mountains experience as discovering its natural phenomena.

Right:
Carrington
Hotel,
Katoomba.

Opposite:
The Zig Zag
Railway from
Lithgow.

BEYOND THE MOUNTAINS

The grandeur of the Blue Mountains extends west to the pastoral serenity of the Megalong Valley and the remote wilderness of Kanangra–Boyd National Park.

Tucked away in a forested valley between the two are the Jenolan Caves. Here, within walls of limestone, time and dripping water have created a secret world remarkable in its extent and beauty.

Visitors accompanied by experienced guides can embark on magical underworld journeys to such evocatively named places as The Temple of Baal, Pool of Cerberus and River Styx.

Opposite:
Intricate limestone formations at Jenolan Caves.

Left:
Caves House, built in 1880.

27

CLIFFS AND VALLEYS

The Blue Mountains region forms a narrow-fingered offshoot of Australia's Great Dividing Range. About 170 million years ago, the mountains were compressed layers of mud and sand beneath a shallow sea. Geological forces gradually raised the seabed into a broad, table-top plateau capped with volcanic basalt. Since that time, the weather and innumerable river tributaries have been carving away the soft sandstones and shales.

The dramatic Blue Mountains landscape of today is but a fleeting apparition in geological time as these same forces return the mountains' ancient sediments to the sea.

Right:
Orphan Rock in the Jamison Valley.

Opposite, top to bottom:
Kanangra Walls and the walking track to Mt Cloudmaker; Grose Valley.

ON THE WILDSIDE

Transport methods old and new offer unique ways to explore the Blue Mountains. For many, the oldest form of transport — footpower — remains the best.

The Great Lithgow Zig Zag Railway, built in the 1860s, still takes steam trains on a spectacular journey featuring viaducts, tunnels and cliffside cuttings.

The adventurous can travel old stock routes in the western valleys on horseback, or abseil down vertical rockfaces for close-up escarpment views. At Katoomba's Scenic World, the Scenic Skyway offers stunning panoramas from 300 metres above the Jamison Valley. The Scenic Cableway makes a thrilling descent to the valley floor, and the Scenic Railway has the steepest incline of any railway in the world.

Right:
A thrilling ride to the valley floor on the Scenic Cableway.

Opposite:
The Scenic Skyway at Katoomba offers magnificent views of the Three Sisters and surrounds.

INDEX

Left:
The Three Sisters look out over the Jamison Valley from Cliff Drive, Katoomba Falls.

Right:
The Superb Lyrebird is a familiar inhabitant of the area.